HOW TO
SPEND
LESS
& Enjoy It More

Dale & Sandy Larsen

INTERVARSITY PRESS
DOWNERS GROVE, ILLINOIS 60515

InterVarsity Press® is the book-publishing division of InterVarsity Christian Fellowship®, a student movement active on campus at hundreds of universities, colleges and schools of nursing in the United States of America, and a member movement of the International Fellowship of Evangelical Students. For information about local and regional activities, write Public Relations Dept., InterVarsity Christian Fellowship, 6400 Schroeder Rd., P.O. Box 7895, Madison, WI 53707-7895.

All Scripture quotations, unless otherwise indicated, are taken from the HOLY BIBLE, NEW INTERNATIONAL VERSION®. NIV®. Copyright ©1973, 1978, 1984 by International Bible Society. Used by permission of Zondervan Publishing House. All rights reserved.

Cover illustration: Marilee Harald-Pilz

ISBN 0-8308-1634-8

Printed in the United States of America

Library of Congress Cataloging-in-Publication Data

Larsen, Dale.
    How to spend less and enjoy it more/Dale & Sandy Larsen.
    p.   cm.
    ISBN 0-8308-1634-8 (alk. paper)
    1. Consumer education.   2. Home economics—Accounting.
3. Finance, Personal—Religious aspects—Christianity.   4. Christian
life—1960-   I. Larsen, Sandy.   II. Title.
TX335.L37 1994   93-42735
640'.73—dc20   CIP

15   14   13   12   11   10   9   8   7   6   5   4   3   2   1

04   03   02   01   00   99   98   97   96   95   94

To the middle-school youth group
Presbyterian-Congregational Church
Ashland, Wisconsin
(see, we didn't forget)

Introduction

If you have less money than you used to, or if for any reason have less money than you think you need, this book is for you. It will help you live *well* on the resources that you have—not someday when you get back on your feet, but now.

By "living well" we mean living enjoyably and even elegantly, free of feeling victimized by circumstances. We'll show you ways to take positive control of a tight situation in five money-eating areas—household, food, clothing, entertainment, and miscellaneous (those general expenses of staying alive).

This book won't scold you for allowing yourself to get into a financial bind. Neither will it show you how to manipulate your way back up to the top of the financial heap by devious power games. And it won't tell you how to invest your last $5 to make a million. It *will* help you live well on less than you might expect—not just by spending less, but by spending creatively and wisely.

For example:

You already know you should turn down the thermostat. We tell you how to turn it *up*—just in time.

You already know you should stop spending so much on entertainment. We help you find—or invent—creative means of free entertainment.

You already know you should cut back on the food bills. We show you how to find equally good food for less money.

So why a Christian book on saving money? Because Christians live in this flawed world and function in the same economy as the rest of society. We are subject to cutbacks and layoffs and shutdowns the same as the rest of the population. We face temptations to feel sorry for ourselves, play revenge games, resent our circumstances, compare ourselves with others, and resort to underhanded means to survive.

Nevertheless, Christians have unique values and resources that help us cope and even flourish in a reduced financial situation.

This is not another "simple lifestyle" book. Yes, the ideas here can help Christians deliberately cut down their spending for daily needs so more of their money can go for causes they want to support. But you'll find ideas for elegant living in these pages. Ideas for entertaining beautifully. Ideas for decorating your home in a way that makes you and your guests feel luxurious about being there. In short, here are 50 imaginative ideas for making the most of a tight financial situation. They'll probably spur you to think of 50—or 150—of your own.

HOUSEHOLD

I

*H*ousing is expensive. Everybody knows that keeping up a home
consumes a huge portion of the yearly budget. No matter how humble
or how luxurious the residence, for most families it's the major expense.

A roof over your head will always be proportionately expensive, but
there are ways to keep the cost from eating you alive while you develop
a home environment where you feel comfortable. Even on limited
resources your home can be a welcoming place, a personal retreat, an
expression of your unique personality and gifts.

Here are some imaginative suggestions for having a home you enjoy
while holding down expenses in maintenance, furnishings, heating,
repairs, decorating, water, and lighting. As you put them into practice
you'll soon be looking around your rooms and finding more ways to
save while you live well.

TRICK YOUR THERMOSTAT
1

Whon Dale was growing up on the farm, his father used to get up at 5:00 every winter morning to shake down the ashes in the wood stove, open the drafts, and add more wood to heat the house. By cutting dead and mature trees on the farm, they had a continuing supply of energy for less than $5 a year.

While many people in the north are still able to heat their homes very cheaply by cutting their own wood, it's impractical for most Americans.

However, there are many ways to keep our heating costs down without growing icicles on our noses. One of the easiest is to turn down the thermostat at night and use a warm comforter, extra blankets, or an electric blanket. As long as you're warm in bed, it doesn't matter how cold the house gets, and the colder it gets the more money you save, right?

The flaw in this scheme is that you have to get up in a cold house to turn the thermostat back up in the morning. It takes less time than it took Dale's dad to get a wood fire going, but it's still unpleasant.

One answer is an automatic setback thermostat, but they start at about $50, which is an expensive way to start saving money. They have another disadvantage for an apartment dweller: If you buy one and install it, you'll probably have to leave it behind when you move on.

A lower-cost solution that accomplishes the same end is putting a lamp with a 100-watt bulb next to the thermostat and plugging the light into a timer, which you possibly already own. This trick works because your thermostat is too dumb to know the difference between the temperature of the house in general and the temperature of the few cubic inches of air around the thermostat.

Leave the lamp on at night, and the heat from the bulb will keep the thermostat warm—and the furnace off. Set the timer so it turns the light off shortly before you want to get up in the morning. The thermostat will feel the sudden cold snap and dutifully turn the furnace back on, allowing the heat to return to normal just in time for you to get up and face your day.

Beats getting up in the cold and shaking down the ashes.

FLIPPING
THE SWITCH
2

*A*s kids we were all reminded to turn off the light whenever we left a room. Cutting your electric bill can be just that easy: consistently flip off the switch. Stated more positively, have lights burning only when and where you need them at the moment.

Yet the light in our home office often stays on all day, even when we're downstairs for lunch or gone for a short time for any reason. Why? We'll tell you in a minute.

Everybody is promoting energy-saving light bulbs, but before you replace all the bulbs in your house, consider how you'll use them and how they work. Some incandescent bulbs described as "energy-efficient" use less electricity by giving less light. You can accomplish the same thing by using smaller bulbs in the first place.

The new compact fluorescent bulbs can be real energy-savers. They cost more but last ten times longer and give four times as much light as incandescents. These bulbs boldly go where no fluorescent tube has gone before, fitting under your lampshades like ordinary incandescent bulbs. But they don't fit all lamp or overhead light fixtures, they can't be used with a dimmer switch, and in three-way lamps they're either on or off.

The compact fluorescents use less energy—*except* where they are frequently switched on for only a short time. This is because fluorescent bulbs eat a jolt of electricity every time they're turned on.

That's why our office light often stays on all day. It's lit with a double-tube fluorescent "shop light." When either of us leaves the office, before we turn off the light we ask, How soon will one of us be back to work there? By switching it off whenever we leave the room for a few minutes, we would actually use more electricity than by leaving it on.

The halogen lights are another good energy saver. These use about 30 percent less energy than incandescent bulbs. Their main advantage over fluorescent lights is their ability to work on a dimmer switch. They are also smaller, so they will go almost anyplace an incandescent bulb will go.

In fixtures with halogen or ordinary incandescent bulbs, which is what most of us have throughout our homes, it's always cheaper to turn off the light than to leave it on. In the end maybe Mom was right; turning off the light is still the best way to cut the electric bill.

BASIC REPAIRS
3

*T*hings break down. Even in the best of homes, things quit working, or they make noises like they're about to go haywire. Expenses rack up quickly if you call an electrician or plumber or handyman every time something quits.

With just a little know-how, many of the little things that go wrong around the house are easy to fix.

Don't panic. You don't have to be a licensed electrician or take your life in your hands to do a simple fix-it job. There's help out there. Two of the most frequently used books in our personal library are both from Reader's Digest: the *Fix-It-Yourself Manual* and the *Complete Do-It-Yourself Manual.* The *Fix-It-Yourself Manual* tells how to repair almost anything around the house. The *Complete Do-It-Yourself Manual* mainly tells how to fix the house itself.

A Sense of Independence

To live well on less we must get things through unusual sources in unusual ways. That means we will sometimes act and look different from the mainstream of America. We won't always be able to join in when coworkers are talking about shopping at the upscale mall or how they cooked last night's sirloin. Living this way requires a sense of independence. Decide that you have the freedom of your own taste. Always ask "What would I like?" instead of "What would So-and-So expect to see me have?"

We live in this world, but this world should not run us. "Don't let the world around you squeeze you into its own mould, but let God re-make you so that your whole attitude of mind is changed" (Romans 12:2 Phillips).

If you're not accustomed to "doing it yourself," start with something simple. One of the easiest beginning projects is the frayed end of a lamp cord next to the plug.

Ready? Unplug the cord and take a close look at it. If it's only cracked or frayed near the plug, cut it off using a wire cutter or by laying it on a piece of wood and using a sharp knife. The cut should be square across the end of the wire.

At the hardware store you will find a collection of various electrical plugs. Among them will be some small plastic ones. For some of these you need only to take a center core out, thread the wire through a hole in the shell, place the end of the wire in a hole in the core, then squeeze the prongs together and snap the core back into the shell. A couple of sharp points in the core pierce the insulation of the wire, making electrical contact.

For heavier cords you will need a larger plug with screw-binding posts. To use one of these, cut off the old plug and separate the two halves of the insulated wire for about two inches. Strip off about an inch of insulation on each. Slip both halves of wire through the shell of the new plug and tie the two halves into a small knot. Wrap the end of each wire around one of the prongs of the plug, form a small loop of bare wire around the screw next to the prong, and tighten with a screwdriver.

When working with wire formed from separate strands, be careful not to leave any loose strands sticking out. It will be easier if you twist the strands together before making the loop. There should be a piece of plastic or paper that slips over the two prongs to cover the wire inside the plug.

Either of the two Reader's Digest books will give you instructions for many money-saving projects around your home. Both are clearly written and well illustrated. Lots of other good do-it-yourself books are also on the market.

We don't promise "You'll never have to call a professional again!" But at least you will have to call less often.

ADD ANOTHER LAYER
4

*I*t's pretty obvious that if you want to be warmer, you should put on more clothes. That's why Eskimos wear fur and South Sea islanders wear next to nothing. But when you're sitting indoors and you start feeling cold, it seems a lot handier to turn up the thermostat than to put on a fur parka.

Stop and think about that. Do you want the house warmer, or do you want yourself and the other people in the house warmer?

You are your own heat-producing plant. Inside, you stay at 98.6° F. You're generating heat by burning up calories just reading this book. So before you raise the temperature of your whole house, think of how to conserve more of your own personal heat.

Here in the north we quickly learn about layering clothes. Outdoors in below-zero weather, it's amazing how much difference one extra pair of socks or one more sweatshirt makes. The additional layer traps air and slows heat conduction.

You don't have to wait until you get cold to put on more layers. If you're already comfortable and you put on more layers, you can turn down the thermostat and still stay comfortable. Now that's a nice thought!

STOP A
COLD WIND
5

*W*e lived in Northern Ireland for a year at the end of a bay between two mountain ranges. At times it seemed the wind was funneled down the bay between the mountains right into our apartment. As we were sitting next to our coal fire one night, the carpet seemed to be moving across the room in waves. A little exploring in the coal room under the apartment revealed a large crack that allowed the wind to blow across the room under the carpet. That's what created the wave action.

You don't need to wait for your carpet to start blowing away to use a cold windy day to find all of those little cracks that waste your heat. A smoldering match or candle will help locate the smallest cracks. Once they are located, all it takes is a quick swipe with a caulking gun to stop them.

When you've finished inside, check the outside of the house for cracks, particularly where the foundation meets the house, around windows and doors, and wherever pipes, vents, and other things go through the walls.

If you have very little to caulk, you can find the caulking in a tube like bathroom caulk and sealer. For larger areas, a cheap caulking gun and regular tubes of caulk will do the job. Except for extreme conditions, you don't need the more expensive high-tech caulks. Some caulks even come in a variety of colors to help make a caulking job inconspicuous. A wet finger or cloth will quickly wipe away any excess caulk, making a neat-looking job.

Of course it would be a lot easier to keep the heat in if we humans didn't have this passion to see the outdoors. That's why we invented windows, and a lot of heat gets lost through them. You can cut down the loss and keep the view by covering the windows with clear plastic. It comes in kits, but buying a clear plastic painting drop cloth is cheaper. Masking tape will hold it in place, though the special clear tape certainly looks better.

Plastic "vee-strip" weather stripping is very effective around doors and older windows. Many newer windows have their own weather stripping system that may need to be checked and replaced.

The vee strips are easy to put around a door. Clean the door frame with alcohol, cut the vee strip to size, remove the backing, and stick it in place with the open side of the vee facing out. (The package includes clear instructions.)

Double-hung windows, where the sashes move up and down, are a little more work because you must remove the wood strip holding the lower sash in place. Drive a stiff putty knife behind the wood strip to pry it off. Then lift the sash clear of the window sill and swing it out. If it has sash ropes, just let it hang from the ropes while you apply the vee strips.

One strip goes on the inside bottom of the upper sash with the open part of the vee down. Two strips go on each side of the window frame. You can use either vee strip or a foam weather strip on the bottom of the lower sash.

Replace the lower sash and tack the wood strip that holds it in place. If you have worked carefully and there weren't too many layers of paint on the window, you may not even have to touch up the paint.

ENERGY-SMART
APPLIANCES
6

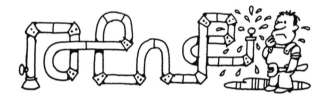

W hen we bought our house, it had an electric water heater. We replaced it with a gas water heater, and a funny thing happened. Our electric bill was cut in half, and our gas bill did not go up an equal amount.

We don't guarantee that you will experience exactly the same savings, but if you have an electric water heater, consider replacing it with gas. Compare costs in your area of the country and investigate what would be involved in installing a gas water heater in your home. Gas water heaters heat water faster than electric, so you can get by with a smaller model. In our case, gas pipes and a vent into the chimney were already in place, but even if we had needed to do the extra work, the gas water heater would have paid for itself. We purchased a used gas heater and sold the electric one.

Obviously this suggestion applies only if you own your home and have control over the type of water heater you use. Switching from electric to gas may not make as big a difference right away in your home as it did in ours. But it's worth considering if you have an electric heater now and want to cut your electric bill. And if your old electric heater needs to be replaced anyway, now is an excellent time to consider gas.

While you're at it, check the efficiency of your refrigerator, furnace and air conditioner.

As a refrigerator ages, its compressor becomes less efficient and has to run longer to keep things cold. In addition, new models are much more energy efficient. It may not pay to replace a refrigerator which cost several hundred dollars just to save a few dollars on your electric bill. However, if your old one is having a hard time keeping things cold or needs repairs, it is well worth considering the possible savings by replacing it.

Since heating your home probably costs you more than your water heater and refrigerator put together, you stand to save the most money by replacing your furnace. If your furnace is quite old, check into the possible savings by replacing it with a newer, high-efficiency furnace.

If air conditioning rather than heating is your major expense, check the possible savings of a newer, more efficient air conditioner. If your old one no longer keeps you as cool as you'd like, you may be able to save money and be more comfortable at the same time.

Also don't forget to check the outside temperature in the evening before leaving the air conditioner on all night. On a cool evening a large fan in the bedroom window will do as much good as an air conditioner—for far less money.

Bonus: If you anticipate selling your home in the near future, that new furnace or air conditioner or water heater will make a good selling point. Our home is for sale right now, and we can boast that it has a new water heater—only because after ten years, that second-hand heater finally rusted out!

IMAGINATIVE DECOR
7

*Y*ou've decided your home needs brightening up. When you consult the home-decorating magazines, they tell you how to landscape your forty-acre front lawn with mature fruit trees and build an octagonal gazebo beside your fish pond. Their interior shots look like Martha Stewart gone on a rampage. What if you don't have the money to work these miracles?

There are inexpensive ways to give your home a facelift. Just changing the furniture around does a lot to give things a fresh feel. Add a few interesting items in places where the eye will find them pleasurable.

By "interesting items" we obviously don't mean fine art of museum quality. We mean . . . well, here are some of the things that add interest to various rooms in our home.

Bathroom:
    two brass quails
    an Old Spice lighthouse decanter
    a foreign stamp in a tiny frame
Living room:
    postcards and note cards in small frames
    attractive old books picked up for twenty-five cents
    a metal hand on a spring for holding letters to mail (hangs
      on the wall)
    a wooden file drawer for three-by-five-inch index cards (it
      holds cassette tapes)
    a large basket for a wastebasket
Kitchen:
    a honey-bear squeeze bottle filled with soap (we call him
      "Soapy the Bear")
    some metal canisters we got with food items inside (like the
      ones with chocolate chips on the 100th anniversary of the
      chocolate chip, or whatever it was)
    old utensils
Bedroom:
    a music stand (thrown away by a church) with a stringless
      violin hanging from it
    necklaces hanging on the wall instead of put away in a
      jewelry box

Where do we find this stuff? Anywhere and everywhere. At garage sales, at stores like Kmart and Wal-Mart, at flea markets. (More about flea markets in the miscellaneous section.)

By the way, check with your public library; some libraries have paintings and small sculptures you can borrow for a few weeks, just like you borrow books. At that rate you could keep a number of interesting items on rotation, and they're all free.

Maybe you wouldn't want any of the items we described in

Remain Generous

While this is a book about spending less, it's not a book about holding on to what we have. There's always a danger, when we realize we have to spend less because we have less to spend, that an attitude of self-protection can take over. The fewer dollars available, the more we think, "We've got to hold on to what we've got."

One of the most famous sayings of Christ is recorded not in the Gospels but in Acts 20:35: "It is more blessed to give than to receive." Part of the beauty of spending less on our everyday living is that we have more to give others.

---

your home. That's fine. We're not living in your house, and you're not living in ours. Decorate *your* home with the items *you* come across that *you* find interesting.

You might even be inspired to write an illustrated article for a home-decorating magazine.

YOUR OWN ALL-PURPOSE CLEANER

8

M ildew was building up on the shower curtain and in the corners of the shower. The "Magic Mildew Remover" was guaranteed to remove it without scrubbing—just spray it on. It cost several dollars for a small spray bottle, but it sure worked like a charm. The mildew was disappearing, but . . . "What's that smell?" Sniff! Sniff! "It sure smells familiar. I wonder. Isn't that . . . ? It smells exactly like . . . chlorine bleach!"

Sure enough, the ingredients listed on the label quickly confirmed our suspicions. We could have bought several gallons of brand-name bleach and a sprayer for the cost of that miraculous little bottle.

Have you noticed how specialized cleaning supplies have become? You could fill a closet with individual cleaners for glass, bathtubs, kitchen floors, bathroom floors, countertops, walls, and window sills.

Consumer Reports published a recipe for a homemade glass cleaner that will clean just about anything. (Don't mix it with bleach, however, because it contains ammonia. Bleach and ammonia in combination release dangerous gases.)

½ cup sudsy ammonia

1 pint alcohol

1 teaspoon liquid dish soap

water to make 1 gallon

Those proportions aren't sacred, so alter them as you wish for cleaning different things. Using less water, of course, makes a more concentrated and powerful solution, useful for spray-bottle targets.

With such a good all-purpose cleaner available for pennies a gallon, you probably expect that our house sparkles all the time. Well, sorry, but this cleaner does not supply either the time or the motivation for cleaning!

ADD LIFE WITH PLANTS
9

*S*everal years ago we were given an avocado pit in the hope that it would sprout. It not only sprouted; it's now a tree that threatens to take over the living room. Sometimes growing three feet in a week, it shoots out branches that hit the ceiling until they get so heavy they bend down to menace whoever is sitting on the couch. We keep cutting it back, and it keeps growing.

The avocado tree fills one corner of the living room. A bay window is adorned with a grape ivy that's been around ten years. On tables and bookcases all over our house, there are green plants, each placed with careful purpose.

If you aren't accustomed to decorating with house plants, you'll be surprised at the life and brightness they bring to your home. Even if you already have plants but keep them all in one spot, you may not have realized their decorating strength throughout the house. Even plants that need a lot of light can be rotated into low-light rooms for a while before they have to go back to the sunnier side of the house.

Maybe you think you have a "brown thumb": if you even look at a plant, it dies. Or your home is dark. Try undemanding low-light plants like one of the philodendrons or spider plants. We have found, like someone said, "plants thrive on tender loving neglect." The plant you forget to water is more likely to survive than the one you over-water. A library book or inexpensive booklet will tell you more about the best plants for your home conditions.

Does acquiring plants sound expensive rather than cheap? Greenhouse owners won't like us, but nobody ever needs to *buy* a house plant (unless you're looking for a particularly unusual kind). Just make it known you'd really like some plants, or admire the lush plants in someone else's home, and people will deluge you with cuttings. Somebody is sure to give you a spider plant they've been praying will die because they're tired of it.

That's another nice thing about plants—they're easily shared and they always remind you of the people who gave them to you.

Plants occasionally get diseases and sometimes have to be thrown out. Don't get weepy; just start over with more cuttings. In fact, the cuttings themselves make attractive house plants while you're rooting them in glasses of water.

When you're going around watering all those plants, you can actually save on your water bill at the same time. You know all the cold water that runs down the drain while you're waiting for the hot water to get hot? Catch it in pitchers and use it to water your plants. Now there's another whole money-saving idea we've thrown in for free.

TWO DESIGNER TOUCHES
10

*I*f you can take what you already own and rearrange it more attractively, you've improved your living space for free.

When we lived in the Chicago area, we had a friend whose little apartment always looked gorgeous. The apartment itself had massive flaws: it was cramped and dark and the wallpaper was buckling. Yet you walked into Jim's place and said "Wow!"

We moved into an unfurnished cottage and for the first time began to decorate from scratch. Like Jim, we had some nice things and scattered them throughout the house, but the effect wasn't as Wow! as his apartment. Finally Sandy asked Jim what made the difference.

He said, "I put things in groups."

What an eye-opener! We had been placing chairs and

pictures and plants here and there, one by one. Jim focused on a location, say a corner or one part of a wall, then grouped a collection of items there. The items didn't have to be similar or related in any way, just as long as they all made a balanced and pleasing unit.

What does grouping things have to do with saving money? If you're short on cash, you've probably had to put off getting that shabby chair reupholstered or the worn carpet replaced. You feel self-conscious about the flaws in your home and think everybody sees them.

By grouping things in eye-satisfying units, you influence the visitor's perception by controlling the visitor's eye (and your own eye while you're at it). Instead of roaming over the room noticing good and bad features equally, the eye is drawn from focal point to focal point, resting on each and enjoying it before being drawn to the next. Careful groupings steer the eye to attractive areas—and away from flaws such as the bad spot in the carpet or the water stain on the wall.

Why Are You Looking for Cheaper Ways to Live?

Because you have to? Because you're poor? Those are negative ways to look at it.

Because you're accomplishing a positive purpose? That's much better!

As you discover and invent ways to live on less, you and your family must know that you're doing this for a reason (and what your reason is). You're not doing it to be martyrs but to gain something: the liberating sense that in the midst of financial hardship, you *have enough*.

While Jim taught us grouping, another friend taught us layering. (Good strategy: if you admire something about somebody else's decor, ask how it was done.) Mo had a houseful of Victorian collectibles like ours. Sandy would come home from a visit determined to make her house more like Mo's—but couldn't. What made the difference?

"I put things in front of things," Mo said.

Another revelation! Our furniture was all pushed back against the four walls; Mo brought chairs and sofas out away from the walls and put higher things behind them, and she put low stands or baskets in front of desks or shelves. The effect was a three-dimensional texture instead of flatness.

Layering can conceal your home's flaws by literally covering them up. You can even layer with cloth remnants. We acquired a buffet that was water damaged and had lost much of its veneer on top. A yard of attractive cloth, split in half lengthwise and sewn together at the ends, covers the top and hides the wreckage. Now that damaged buffet even gets compliments!

FOOD
II

*E*verybody has to eat. That's right. Food is getting more expensive. That's right, too. You have a low income right now, so you have to live on low-quality food. Good news—that's wrong.

When we grumble about the high cost of eating, a little perspective helps. We are blessed to live in a part of the world where good food is available in abundance and in great variety.

Shortly after completing this book, if all goes as planned, we will be going to live in Russia where the food situation is much different. One person who visited a city in northern Russia said that she cried when she came back and went into an American grocery store.

We don't say that to make us all feel guilty, but to demonstrate that things aren't always as tight as they feel. In our society, one hour's work at minimum wage will buy about eight pounds of rice, or several pounds of beef, or a couple of whole chickens—easily enough to feed a family for a day. Compared with much of the world, we put in very little work for the food we need.

Of course, for us, food reflects fun as well as work. Food does more *than nourish us for another day. It brings people together for special occasions. Can you think of a single holiday that doesn't have some kind of food associated with it? Even the taste or smell of a particular food can bring back warm memories. Cotton candy, grilled hamburgers, warm chocolate chip cookies, butter melting on an ear of corn—it all has meaning beyond our bodies' need for fuel.*

We'll tell you how we enjoy cooking and eating while being prudent at the grocery store. We'll also share some ways to avoid the grocery store entirely.

NATURAL-FOODS STORES
11

Go into your local organic food store and take a deep breath. The mingled aromas of spices, coffees, grains, and fruits will tantalize you. You've never seen these brand names and logos in TV commercials. Many items aren't even in packages on shelves. They're in bins with scoops, and you bag your own.

The best savings here are likely to be the bulk items such as spices, loose teas, beans, and grains like oatmeal; they're often astronomically cheaper than at the grocery stores. Canned goods and produce, however, are typically more expensive.

While some people "naturally" gravitate toward natural-foods places, other people shy away from them because of their image. When Sandy recommended the local food co-op to one lady, she asked warily, "Isn't that a hippie place?"

Well, yes and no. They sometimes have that look of casual earthiness, which may be positive or negative in your mind. Or they may gleam like the typical chain grocery store.

That brings us to the important distinction that not all "natural-foods" stores are the same. Some ask you to pay premium prices for everything. As with all your shopping, if you want to be sure to save money, you'll need to take the time to jot down prices and compare costs at the various stores available.

Some natural-foods stores are co-ops where you can get a further discount if you put in a few hours a month working at the store (clerking, stocking shelves, unloading the truck and so forth). But even if you just go in and buy a few bulk items, a visit to the offbeat atmosphere of the natural-foods store is a refreshing change from the typical chain grocery store.

MARKED-DOWN
CARTS
12

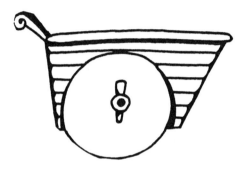

*D*oes your grocery store have a bin or cart with marked-down merchandise? Dented cans, slightly crushed boxes, bottles with torn labels, items they've stopped stocking? Scout this out. Prices are usually cut in half. If only the package is damaged—not the food—and if it isn't something perishable, it's probably a good deal. The contents of this bin change constantly, so you never know what you'll find there. It might be something you've thought of trying, but the regular price is too high. Or it might be something you need for a particular meal.

Sometimes I'll have a recipe that calls for some particularly unusual canned or bottled ingredient that's more than I want to pay. If I watch, this item will often turn up in the bargain cart, and that's the week I'll make that recipe.

Are you embarrassed to be seen sorting through the damaged stuff in the marked-down bin? Here's where the independence we talk about so much comes in. Don't look around to see who's watching; just do it and go on. Actually you're being smart. If the contents of the damaged packages are as good as what's in the undamaged packages, it makes no sense to pay the full price.

CO-OP FOOD PROGRAMS
13

*E*very month a truck pulls up at the Bohemian Hall, where volunteers are waiting to unload crates of fruit, sacks of potatoes, cartons of frozen meat, boxes of colorful vegetables. For the next hour or so, a dozen people work to bag the food in small amounts and arrange it on long tables. The buyers are already arriving with their boxes. Earlier in the month they signed up and paid $14.50. Now they push their boxes along the tables while packers load them: five pounds of potatoes, a bag of tangerines, a head of lettuce, five pounds of frozen chicken, and so forth till the box is almost too heavy to lift. In the grocery store this food would have cost more than twice as much.

This isn't welfare or a government handout. This is Fare

Share, a cooperative food-buying organization. When you sign up each month, you don't know exactly what you're going to get, but there's always meat, fruit, vegetables, pasta, cereals, sometimes canned goods and a few miscellaneous packaged items.

Fare Share makes sense if what you get is what you would have bought in the store anyway. There's always the risk that you or your family might not like something you get, but you risk that any time you buy a new item.

Fare Share happens to be the food buying co-op in our area. Many other cooperative arrangements can be found across the country. If none exists in your area, you might try forming your own with the cooperation of a few friends and a little research.

The eyes of all look to you,
  and you give them their food at the proper time.
You open your hand
  and satisfy the desires of every living thing.
(Psalm 145:15-16)

FANCY MEALS FOR LESS
14

Y ou don't have to sit down to a can of beans to have an inexpensive meal. Even on a tight food budget, you can still enjoy some of the fancy meals from your gourmet cookbooks (you know, the ones you bought before you lost your job).

The secret lies in the happy fact that nobody is looking over your shoulder making sure you really use veal steaks or sour cream or shallots. You can substitute similar but less expensive ingredients and come up with basically the same dish. (Hardcore gourmets won't agree with this, but they have skipped this section anyway.)

Go through your recipes, or a library cookbook, and experiment with substituting. You'll save the most in the meat recipes, by using a cheaper cut of meat or a different meat

Avoiding the Poverty Syndrome

Living *well* on less means that because you spend a little less here and there, you can afford a small luxury or indulgence now and then *while* you actually enjoy the process of saving the money needed for it.

Concentrating on low-cost ways to add elegance means you feel more luxurious and less deprived even while you spend less. Each act of low-cost elegance frees a little bit of money for something else, without your going into the poverty syndrome in the meantime. You don't have to live on bread and water for a week before you do something nice. You can enjoy saving the money to spend on something else you enjoy.

entirely—and by using less of it.

Another way to make a plain meal fancy is the creative use of herbs and spices. Don't be afraid to use them liberally. Unlike salt, you can't ruin a dish with too many herbs. Honest.

As with all the suggestions in this book, you can commit yourself to substituting cheaper ingredients without being a slave to them. If you want to get some more expensive foods now and then for a special meal, go ahead. Nobody is going to arrest you for buying butterhead lettuce or kiwi fruit. Just make a general practice of using less expensive foods.

By the way, if you need to eat the very cheapest for a while but still get balanced nutrition, build your meals on eggs, carrots, cabbage, rice and apples. From our nonscientific survey over the past twenty years, those are consistently the cheapest foods. You could .add oatmeal and skim milk for breakfast. If you'd rather avoid eggs, go for poultry or fish (frozen or fresh fillets, not packaged and breaded).

INEXPENSIVE SNACKS
15

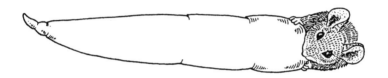

*T*here's a huge price range in snack foods, and if you use them a lot, it makes sense to go for the less expensive. For example:

Popcorn. If you're bored with the taste, try seasoned salt or pepper or other flavorings. The bagged store brands of un-popped corn are the most economical. It's true that not all the kernels will pop. But considering that you pay about four times as much for the high-class brand, you pay a lot per kernel to get those last few kernels popped. You don't have an air popper? Or it melted last New Year's Eve? Shaking a pan over the fire, which worked fine before the Pilgrims landed, still gets good results.

Toast and jam. (If it's homemade jam on toasted homemade

bread, you're almost in heaven.)

Cheese. A good piece of cheese is as good on a saltine as on a gourmet cracker, which costs you more per pound than the cheese.

Mixes of pretzels, nuts, cereals and the like. It doesn't have to be the standard brand-name party mix. You can use cheaper cereals like generic "O's."

Will these low-cost snacks really make a difference in your spending? It depends on how much you snack. If you're one person occasionally having a late-night nibble, it doesn't add up to much, so don't feel guilty about the price tag on that bag of gourmet mesquite-flavored blue corn chips. If you're a family of five raiding the kitchen at all hours of the day and night, then, yes, it makes a big difference.

CASSEROLE SAVVY
16

Sandy once argued with her friend from North Dakota over the meaning of "hot dish." Louise had cooked something and when Sandy asked what it was, the answer was "It's a hot dish" (pronounced HOTdish). Any fool could see it was hot; it was steaming. But what was it? Further research showed that *hot dish* is the Scandinavian-American term for casserole (otherwise known as tureen, covered dish, and probably fifty other local terms). It might also be called "what you always bring to a church potluck."

Casseroles are famous for stretching a small amount of meat a long way. A casserole can transform two pieces of leftover chicken or half a pound of hamburger into dinner for the whole family.

The catch is that most casserole recipes want you to bind everything together with canned condensed soup (usually cream of mushroom, cream of celery, or cream of chicken). The price of that can of soup often comes to more than the meat, and the meat is already expensive enough.

Condensed cream soup does appear to work magic in casseroles, but if you read the label on the can, there's nothing magical about it. Canned soup is flavored broth (highly salted) plus milk, thickener, and fat, plus a very small amount of vegetable or meat to make it "cream of" mushroom or chicken or whatever.

Those few ounces of ingredients don't have to come out of an expensive can; add them yourself and accomplish the same magic in your next casserole.

If you make a lot of casseroles, especially large ones, it's handy to have your own dry "canned-soup" mix ready and waiting. This basic recipe, equivalent to nine cans of condensed soup, is a simplified version of a recipe in a Fare Share newsletter:

  2 cups dry nonfat milk (get the generic or store brand)
  ¾ cup cornstarch
  ¼ cup dry bouillon—chicken, beef, vegetable, or any flavor
    (buy it in bulk rather than the cubes)
  any seasonings you want (salt, pepper, onion flakes, thyme,
    oregano, garlic powder)

Keep the mix in a tightly lidded jar. To substitute for one can of condensed soup, combine ⅓ cup of the dry mix with 1 ¼ cups of water. You can cook the reconstituted mix till it thickens before you add it to the casserole, or you can just add the mix and water to the other ingredients.

If you want, add a tablespoon of butter or margarine. Half a stick of celery or a few canned or fresh mushrooms or a small amount of any vegetable will make it into "cream of . . ." whatever you choose, but your casserole probably already contains other vegetables and meat.

Easy, right? That wasn't magic; that was being smart.

MAKE MORE FROM SCRATCH
17

*T*he idea behind that canned-soup substitute is applicable to a lot of prepackaged foods. If you're in the habit of using "convenience" foods, why not experiment with preparing more meals from scratch? You're bound to spend less on groceries, and you'll probably enjoy eating—and cooking—more.

Before you skip this section saying "I can't cook!" first read it once. It really is surprisingly easy to make your own inexpensive versions of all kinds of "convenience" foods. You can make them with less fat and salt or anything else you don't want, and you can put into them exactly what you choose. Read the label, estimate roughly how much of each basic ingredient there must be in the package, and go home and try making your own. It does not have to be exactly like the store-bought to be a success. You may like your own version better.

Some people balk at making meals from scratch because they think it takes longer. Sometimes it does. On the other hand, some "convenience" foods aren't all that convenient, and their small amount of convenience comes at a high price.

For example, "minute" rice costs about a dollar more per pound than regular rice, and the package instructs you to let it sit for five minutes after it boils. You can cook regular short-grain rice in ten minutes. At a dollar extra for saving you five minutes, the rice is earning $12 an hour.

Likewise, the expensive boxed meat "helpers" tell you to cook their prepackaged pasta or potatoes or rice for anywhere from ten to thirty minutes—or exactly as long as it would take to cook the same thing bought in a big bag.

Flexibility Equals Freedom

If you're a little afraid of experimentation in the kitchen, keep in mind that experimentation is the soul of living on less. If your economic situation has changed, you'll survive by being flexible enough to change with it. Instead of clinging to the way things were, look to the way things can be. If you can't have the things you had before or do the things you did before, then your freedom lies in having and doing different things.

While you *can* spend all day cooking one meal from scratch, cooking with basic ingredients does not have to take enormous amounts of your time. For example (assuming the meat is not frozen), you can go into the kitchen, start potatoes or rice cooking, put a chuck steak on to broil, cook a vegetable, make a salad, and sit down at the table to less than half an hour.

Another quick meal from scratch is to put rice or noodles on, then fry any ground meat (hamburger, turkey, pork) and add any vegetables you have lurking around the refrigerator. Mix in the cooked rice or serve it separately.

Yes, you could buy a similar meal in microwaveable packages and save some time, but they would cost far more, and they wouldn't taste like fresh food. They would save you clean-up time, yet you'd also throw away a lot of wasted packaging. But that's getting into another issue.

STOCKPILE OR STRETCH IT OUT?

18

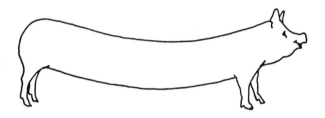

*T*here are two philosophies about how to do your food shopping so you make the most efficient use of your money. Both require planning, and since impulse buying is the death of your grocery budget, each is wise in its own way.

According to one school of thought, each week you should buy as few groceries as possible. A full larder ties up spending money you might need, so don't buy a single thing until the week you need it. Unspent money, still in your bank account, is earning interest, while food sitting on the shelf is just getting older. "Bare-bones" shopping carries the pleasure of walking through the store knowing that you don't need most of what you're looking at. Its big disadvantage is you'll run close to the edge and may occasionally get caught short of something.

The other school of thought in food shopping says that when there's an excellent sale on a food you use regularly, buy a large quantity and stockpile it. (Obviously, this applies only to nonperishable foods or foods you have room to freeze.) If there's a terrific sale on canned corn and you buy six months' supply, for your budget it's as though the sale price lasted six months. Some weeks you'll spend more, but many weeks you'll find yourself eating out of your food store instead of the grocery store. The disadvantage is that you have to find a place to store all those cans and boxes. Your closets and spare bedroom may start to look like you're expecting an alien siege. You *may* be besieged—by mice or bugs—if you store things like pancake mixes and cake mixes; canned goods are safer.

In our home we practice the first kind of food shopping, trying to buy only what's needed very soon. Sometimes it causes minor crises. This has become a standard joke (or is it a joke?) in our house. Dale: "We're out of . . ." Sandy: "It's on the list." Dale: "I can't eat lists." (Maybe that's not such a joke after all.)

CANDLES AND CLOTH NAPKINS
19

What are these doing in the food section? No, we're not recommending that you start eating wax and fabric. They're here because meals are not just food; meals are a *mood*. Candles and cloth napkins on the table add a lot of elegance to the simplest meal.

Some candles are very costly. But you can get cheap ones at three or four for a dollar, and they add just as much elegance as the expensive ones. Candles on the table set an atmosphere that says "This meal means something. These people are important. Even if for only a few minutes, we're carving out a time and place where our lives slow down and we enjoy the present."

Maybe you don't care for candlelight when you eat. Then

think of what *would* add a touch of class to your home's eating place. A small vase with one silk flower? Nice music playing instead of the TV blaring the latest world crisis?

In spite of many other elegant touches on our table, and in spite of our having written a book on ecology, it took a long time for us to switch from paper napkins to cloth. Sandy thought they were expensive and we'd have to own dozens because they'd have to be washed constantly. We had never checked the price of inexpensive cloth napkins or added up what we were spending per year on even the cheapest paper napkins. She was surprised to find that we could buy a dozen cloth napkins, use them for a year and then throw them away or turn them into rags—and still spend less than a year's worth of paper napkins.

But why buy napkins ready-made? If you can sew a straight seam, you can easily make a whole repertoire of stunning cloth napkins from fabric remnants. Dark prints have the advantage of hiding stains the best, besides looking the most elegant. A yard of 45-inch-wide fabric will yield six generous-sized napkins. They don't have to be square, the fabric can have a one-sided print, and not everybody at the table has to have the identical napkin.

If candles and cloth napkins seem inappropriate for homes

> Better a little with the fear of the LORD
>   than great wealth with turmoil.
> Better a meal of vegetables where there is love
>   than a fattened calf with hatred.
> (Proverbs 15:16-17)

with small children, you may want to find some other ways to add a little elegance. But we do know people with young children who usc these touches regularly. In fact their kids seem to have grown up with mealtime being a special time they enjoy together.

USDA
COMMODITIES
AND MORE
20

*T*o support farm prices, the U.S. Department of Agriculture buys surplus farm products and distributes them to people with low incomes. The qualifying income requirement depends on family size and is rather low, but you are evaluated by your average monthly income so far that year. So if your income has taken a recent plunge, you may qualify to get commodities. If your income is very erratic, you may qualify at certain times of the year.

The idea of standing in line for government food handouts goes against an independent nature, and we've stressed an independent nature throughout this book. But independence also means we're free to do things other people might look down on. Why pass up the chance to receive free peanut butter, dry milk, tinned meats, canned fruits and vegetables, cheese, flour, or whatever is available at a commodities distribution?

It's not even inferior food. The quality of the food is excellent because you get it earlier in the food-processing chain, before commercial food manufacturers have had a chance to stretch and dilute it.

Consider other food programs for which you might qualify, such as food stamps. The drawback of all government programs, and the reason many Christians don't like to use them, is that they strike at our sense of pride and self-sufficiency. They also seem like an admission that God hasn't been taking care of us.

While we don't enjoy using these programs and have tended to shy away from them even when we qualify, they can be lifesavers when money is low. None of them is very stimulating to the ego, but as Christians we don't draw our worth or meaning from what people in the grocery store check-out line think of us. Perhaps this is how God has chosen to provide for us at this particular time.

BAKERY
OUTLETS
21

*I*n Jesus' time, bread was so basic to human life that he called himself the "bread of life" (John 6:35, 48) and he chose bread as the enduring symbol of his crucified body (Luke 22:19). Throughout human history, nearly every culture has eaten some kind of bread.

Though bread isn't as central to our diets as it was for the people in Jesus' time, most of us still eat a lot of it. It's been a lunch necessity since the Earl of Sandwich put his meat between two slices of bread so he could stand longer at the gaming tables.

If you live in at least a medium-sized city and your family eats a lot of bakery products, check out the bakery outlets. You can stock up on a week's supply of bakery goods there and save a lot of money. Supposedly it's "day-old" bread, but that's not so bad; the bread in the grocery stores can sit on the shelves for a week.

Clothing

III

Besides needing clothes to keep warm, we've needed them ever since the Fall to make ourselves presentable in society. And not just any old rags will do. Our clothes communicate various messages about ourselves—our identity, our moods, our commitment to creativity or conformity, our degree of respect for ourselves and others.

Of course your clothing demands have a lot to do with your life situation. If you have a job that requires you to be a sharp dresser, or have several children going through simultaneous growth spurts, or have teenagers who will wear only the latest, then finding inexpensive clothing is a challenge—far more than if you're a single wood-carver working in an isolated shop. But anyone, wood-carver or executive secretary, can find less expensive clothes. Here are some ideas about where to look.

GARAGE SALES
22

We once took a Japanese guest to some American garage sales, a phenomenon he had never seen. This would never happen in Japan, he said. People would be too embarrassed to put their used possessions out on the lawn for everyone to see, and no one would want to buy what someone else had already used. In a letter to us after he went home, he wrote that garage sales were "an interesting display of American pragmatism."

Pragmatic, maybe. Cheap, yes. When it comes to second-hand clothing, be glad this isn't Japan. Garage sales (or yard sales, or porch sales, or rummage sales, or moving sales, or whatever they're called in your part of the country) make great sense, especially for kids' clothes. After all, how long do children wear their clothes before they outgrow them? Sometimes they're almost new when they arrive at the sale table.

Garage-sale clothes make sense for adults too. A lot of people buy beautiful new clothes, decide they don't like them after all, let them hang in the closet for a while, then get tired of looking at them and get rid of them in a sale. At some garage sales you'll find new clothes with the tags still on them.

If the price still seems too high, never be afraid to offer a lower price. Just say, "Will you take (name your price) for this?" They might say "Sure!" or you might have to try a little harder to reach a compromise with them.

Also remember that people do not have garage sales to get rich; they have them to get rid of stuff. If you like a lot of things at the sale, pile them up and offer a total price.

The cardinal rule for garage-saling is go early. The best stuff is usually gone by 10:00 a.m. (Of course if you're an unusual size, you'll have a better chance something will still be around.) Occasionally, the good stuff is gone before the sale officially starts because the sellers allow people to buy early. These buyers and sellers are unsportsmanlike players and should be sent to the penalty box.

Are garage-sale clothes inexpensive? Ridiculously inexpensive. Sandy got a . . . well, she won't bore you by telling you what she got. Be warned, though, that if you buy a lot of clothes at garage sales, you may turn into a Boring Garage-Sale Bragger and get your full-length down coat (like new, $8) stuffed down your throat.

RESALE SHOPS
23

*I*n downtown Duluth there's a store called Ragstock, probably one of the most interesting clothing stores you could ever visit. Packed onto racks are coats, sweaters, jeans, suits, kimonos, blazers, hats, even ties and suspenders. Most of it is secondhand, though there are some unique new items (like surplus Swedish Army knickers). Ragstock has a certain deliberate ambience: loud music, racks packed so tightly you can barely walk between them, a bend toward the unusual. The clothes are clean (though never ironed) and we have both found beautiful things there—Dale a winter coat, Sandy several blouses, a skirt, a lightweight coat. The prices were higher than garage-sale prices but far lower than new clothing. Ragstock is a type of the used-clothing-as-chic store.

Another approach to selling used clothing is the *consignment shop*. You'll find great ones in obscure places, such as the huge one we discovered far up on the Keweenaw peninsula in Hancock, Michigan. People place their clothing (and other items) in consignment shops to be sold for a fee. The quality and styles are mixed, since it all depends on who wants to sell what right then. In Hancock the prices were lower than at Ragstock: for example, a raincoat for $3.00 and a blouse for $1.50.

A third kind of used-clothing store is the *thrift shop run for charity*, such as Goodwill, the Salvation Army or, in our town, the SOS Mission run by a local church. These are usually the drabbest of the resale stores, and they tend to get donations of everything that didn't sell at garage sales. (We've done it ourselves.) On the other hand they also receive high-quality clothing from generous well-off people.

Why Not Worry About Clothes?

"Why do you worry about clothes?" (Matthew 6:28).

Why would Jesus ask a question with such an obvious answer? Clothes are a necessity, so who wouldn't get worried when the clothes we need skyrocket beyond our price range? Jesus answered his own question. He didn't say "Forget about clothes"; he just assured us that God knows what we need garment-wise and will provide it one way or the other, once we get our focus off our wardrobes and on to living God's way. He spoke as a man who knows. He was God living on earth—God himself in daily need of clothing, food and shelter.

At one of our local thrift shops Sandy picked up three pairs of dress sandals that looked like they'd never been worn. Price: seventy-five cents each. The charity resale shops have two purposes: they raise money for the work of the sponsoring organization, and they make items available at unusually low prices for people who don't have much to spend. That raises an ethical question: If you buy clothing from the Salvation Army when you don't really have to, aren't you taking away from people who truly are in poverty? That's a matter for your own conscience, but it might be more worrisome if used clothing were at a premium. As it is, these shops are always flooded with it. In America, fashion and whim keep the supply of used clothing coming.

END-OF-SEASON SALES
24

*L*ong before the snow flies, winter coats start appearing on the racks. Then while you're still tracking slush into the store, the swimsuits appear. Those clothing displays are designed to get you thinking ahead and buying what you need well in advance of the season.

In a way it sounds like good planning. When the new season's clothes come into the stores, that's the most appealing time to buy. However, that's not the most economical time to buy. If you wait till the end-of-season sales, you can buy clothes much more reasonably, plus you get to wear them right away instead of waiting for the next season to roll around. It sounds a little risky to wait till the end of the season because things are picked over by then. But when you think how early the next season's stuff appears, the end-of-season sales aren't so late after all.

Of course if you wait till the end of the season to buy that season's clothes, you will not be the first person on your block or in your church who's wearing the very latest. That may or may not matter to you, and if it matters some, you can always buy one or two things at the beginning of the season. Nothing in any of our save-money schemes is meant to be legalistic. Modify these ideas to fit your circumstances and preferences.

With a little more patience, if you wait till next year, some of those fashions will show up in your neighbors' garage sales at one-tenth the price of the end-of-season sales!

WHEN EXPENSIVE IS CHEAPER
25

*T*here are times when it's more costly to try to save money on clothes. That's especially true with buying cheap shoes.

Five years ago, for about $45, Dale bought a pair of good dress shoes at a store that featured discontinued name-brand shoes. Right now the heels are getting worn, but otherwise the shoes still look nearly new. Putting on new heels and half-soles will cost about $25 and should extend their life for another five years. But even if they lasted only eight years, they would cost less than buying $12.95 shoes which last only a year. The cost of continuing to buy the cheap shoes every year would be over $100, while the more expensive shoes would cost only $70. You not only get the savings; you get all those years of extra comfort, since the high-quality shoes just feel better.

Planning ahead means weighing the total value of a piece of clothing over its projected life. Planning also means considering clothing combinations.

If you buy a flamboyant item that goes with maybe one other article in your wardrobe, you've purchased something with very limited use. If you buy a number of items within one color "family," you can interchange them and use them in various combinations. That way you've not only added to but multiplied your wardrobe. Otherwise you'll probably wind up shopping for other things to go with that butter-yellow shirt.

Of course if you want to buy something flamboyant and impractical once in a while, no one will condemn you. Just use wisdom and weigh its dollar value against the enjoyment you'll derive from it—and don't splurge that way too often.

What's Good About Control?

In order to live on less and enjoy it, you must have a desire to take control of your life. The minute you find yourself shopping in a secondhand store and thinking, "Poor me that I'm forced to do this," your strategy is sabotaged. You can't let yourself feel like a victim. Your financial circumstances are not in control; you are in control.

Is being in control of our own lives a Christian way of thinking?

If it means thinking of ourselves as little gods, no.

If it means living as a free person under God, yes. We can live free of the fatalistic sense that life is just happening to us and we're powerless to do anything about it. We can act independently because we have within us the God who is really in charge.

GOING OUT OF BUSINESS...
26

*H*ave you ever seen a store with a permanent going-out-of-business sign? It was there five years ago, and it will stay up until the store goes out of business for real.

Sadly for the store, but fortunately for you, every now and then the going-out-of-business sign is true. If a clothing store really is selling off everything prior to closing, get yourself in there. This is a great chance to get clothes at excellent prices. Since this is a one-time chance, buy for your future needs. If you have young children, stock up on kids' clothes that they'll grow into.

Steel yourself for a different kind of shopping. Be prepared for a competitive crowd and harried clerks. A lot of people want to save money as much as you do, and even if you escape being trampled, you may be disappointed when you go back to take another look at that suede jacket. (It was there five minutes ago!)

You may choose to play the price-reduction lottery. A store selling off everything will often mark down items by a certain percentage each day. So that suit you've got your eye on may be even less tomorrow. Or it may be gone. Should you buy it today or take a chance on tomorrow? Who knows? That's the risk of a going-out-of-business sale, but those of us committed to living on less are used to taking a few risks.

Entertainment
IV

*W*e don't have to be bored just because we don't have much money. Besides, a lot of rich people are bored, which proves money isn't the cure for boredom. We can do endless low-cost things for entertainment.

When we think of entertainment, most of us automatically think of paying to see or do something that someone else provides for our pleasure. Professional sports, movies, concerts, water slides, theme parks—they all entertain us (or at least we go to them hoping they will).

Most of those popular forms of packaged entertainment cost a lot of money. On a limited budget you may have to forgo some of them. At that point it's tempting to revert to childhood and whine, "I don't have anything to do. I'm bored."

But what's entertainment? It's anything you find entertaining. It's whatever gives you a pleasurable diversion from your ordinary routine.

You could spend all the rest of the leisure time of your life discovering pleasurable things that don't cost much—many that are even free. They take imagination, but isn't that better than having someone hand you their version of prepackaged fun?

Beach or Park Parties
27

We had planned a group cookout by the Northwestern University campus on the shore of Lake Michigan. We thought it looked like rain, but a fog was rolling in, and our friend Joe insisted that it couldn't rain when it was foggy. An hour later our fire hissed and sputtered and smoked as the raindrops put it out. Meanwhile, Joe, still insisting it couldn't rain, stood there with water dripping off his nose, asking, "Doesn't anybody want another hot dog?"

The group fled to our house and lit a fire in the fireplace to warm up and dry out. Before long our neighbor started banging on the door. She had smelled wood smoke, and since nobody lights a fire in the fireplace in July, she thought our house was on fire.

Now only a grouch would call that cookout a flop. It was memorable and funny, and it came to such a colorful ending. In fact it's very hard for this kind of party to flop.

Appearances Aren't Everything
One man pretends to be rich, yet has nothing;
another pretends to be poor, yet has great wealth.
(Proverbs 13:7)

Organizing a get-together at a public place is a great way to entertain others. It doesn't cost you any more than you'd spend anyway to feed yourself, and it doesn't matter if your backyard isn't big enough to play hopscotch and you've sold off all your furniture to pay the light bill. Just suggest a beach party or a park party. All you have to do is tell people when and where to show up. The "guests" all bring their own food, some will bring grills, and somebody is bound to come up with some recreation equipment like a volleyball and net. By all means, bring a Frisbee or two. If you're on a beach of any sort, you can swim or sunbathe.

Families appreciate this kind of "dinner invitation" because they don't have to get a sitter or worry that their kids will break your china. It's also a great way to introduce your non-Christian friends to people from your fellowship, because it's fun, it's in neutral territory, and it's a nonthreatening atmosphere.

Be the organizer of outdoor group get-togethers, and you'll be a very popular "host."

NATURAL WONDER
28

Wile camping at a farm where Dale was helping with harvest, Sandy wandered across a hilltop to a pond that had been made for some beehives. Circling the small remote pond was a path, beaten hard as a cement sidewalk.

Human beings had not made that path. There weren't any farm animals in that field. The path had been made by wild animals who were constant visitors to the water. In broad daylight they were nowhere to be seen, but clearly at night the pond was the center of a whole society. At the very edge of the pond, just under the edge of the water, some of their tracks were still visible in the mud.

Oddly enough, the people who lived on the farm had never noticed the path. But Sandy saw it the first time she visited the pond. She had eyes to see it.

Much of our entertainment consists of observing things. We watch TV, we watch football, we watch people flying kites. We choose what we will observe and find entertaining. Observing natural things can be fascinating—and free.

You don't have to take a wilderness vacation to observe the natural world. Have you ever noticed what animals live in your backyard? In the local park? What *was* that funny-looking bug crawling along the sidewalk this morning? Do you have any idea what kinds of wildflowers grow within a quarter mile of your home? How are the clouds today different from yesterday, and what do they tell you about tomorrow's weather?

Helping children see and appreciate God's creation is a great way to grow Christian environmentalists. They will care about God's earth with a biblical perspective because they have come to know both him and that world intimately.

Be prepared: nature is not always nice. You and your children will not spend much time in the field before you see some nasty things. You will see death as well as life. You'll be reminded that nature is not a silkscreen picture on a "Save the Whales" T-shirt, but is a fallen place. That can lead to discussions about sin and about Christ coming into this fallen world to be our Savior.

Your library will have field guides to trees, flowers, birds, mammals, insects and so forth. Binoculars are helpful but not mandatory. A camera is great, but so is a notebook. Go out the door, and see what you can see.

GAME NIGHT
29

W hen was the last time you played Monopoly? How about Clue? Or Scrabble or Pictionary or Scattergories? Invite people (or ask if someone else will let people come) for a game night. You don't all have to agree on the same game; have several going at once. Or have several people bring the same game and turn the evening into, say, a Scruples marathon.

Just about everybody has games in the closet, and some people are glad to bring their own card tables. The coffee table, the kitchen table, and the floor are fine too—and they feel less formal than card tables. (Believe it or not, you don't have to have wall-to-wall carpeting in order to be comfortable sitting on the floor.)

Don't be surprised if many people's games and card tables

are dusty. You're sure to hear several guests say that this is the first time in years they've played board games with other adults, and they'd forgotten how much fun it is.

If the games lag, it's not a disaster. In fact that may be the best part of the evening, because that's when people start to talk. Like many of the ideas in this book, a game night is a good chance to introduce non-Christians to your church friends. (Just don't invite any church friends who are poor sports or lose their tempers when they lose a game!)

POTLUCKS
30

Whenen we were living in the Chicago area on practically nothing, we discovered that a great low-cost way to entertain was to host a potluck. We would make a list of people—maybe all the young couples in our small church, or miscellaneous people we thought would make an interesting combination, or people we wanted to meet each other for any reason—and we invited them to come and bring a dish.

Potlucks can be as organized or as chancy as you want to make them. True pot *luck* means you ask people to bring anything and take your chances that you'll get something besides ten angel food cakes. If you don't like to live quite that dangerously, ask different people to bring an appetizer, salad, vegetable, main course and dessert.

Another way to plan an orderly group meal is to ask people to bring individual ingredients and make one dish together—say pizza or tacos, or crepes (you do the crepes and they bring the fillings). Even a soup-and-sandwich party can be elegant when people bring their favorite homemade soups and sandwich fillings. For example:

We're having a pizza party!

Please bring:

___ sauce

_x_ cheese

___ mushrooms

___ pepperoni

Yes, People Are Busy

You can serve others by hosting or organizing get-togethers like we've suggested. But if you're new to this kind of entertaining, be prepared to hear over and over how busy people are and that it's a nice idea but they can't fit it into their schedule.

Don't take it personally that they don't want to come to your home. Whatever people are doing these days, it isn't leaving them much time to get together in each other's homes. They often want to, but they can't find the time. Keep trying. Invite somebody else. Ask someone in the church or at work that you don't even know. This can become a great ministry to newcomers in your church or community.

You don't have to have a dining table with three leaves to seat an army. Most people are not offended by eating while sitting on the couch or even the floor, so long as you have trays or a coffee table or some way to keep from spilling their food. If you don't have enough silverware or plates for a large group, you can limit your guests to the number you can handle, or you could get some dime-store silverware and reuseable plastic plates.

There is something about the informality and group spirit of these parties that makes people not notice, or not care, if your house isn't perfect. You'll have some expense in putting together this kind of party, but don't worry—it's likely to be balanced by all the leftover food that people don't want to take home. They'll insist you keep it.

IS SPECIAL EQUIPMENT NECESSARY?

31

*I*f you're used to high-cost recreation, cutting your entertainment cost means learning some new and different things to do for fun. A lot of people would like to learn new recreational skills, but they're inhibited by the expense of buying all the equipment.

The truth is that you can do a lot of recreational activities and sports without looking like the people in the beer commercials. For the equipment you do need, there are less expensive sources than high-end sporting-goods shops.

The guiding principle is *get what you really need*, not what the popular image of the activity demands. As examples, we'll tell you how we do our favorite winter and summer recreational activities. Obviously our examples reflect our interests and area of the country, but you can adopt the same principle to the activities that interest you.

In winter we cross-country ski often, sometimes several times a week. Most people think skiing is an expensive sport. Everybody you see in the pictures is wearing racy neon jackets and pants, special sunglasses, head gear, nose warmers. But you do not need these. We ski in blue jeans and always have. In fact our standard outfit for below-zero cross-country skiing is long underwear (top and bottom), light socks under heavy socks, jeans, t-shirt, two sweatshirts and a light nylon jacket, a scarf, stocking cap and mittens. All these are ordinary clothes that anybody in a cold climate already owns. By the end of the run we're usually shedding some of those clothes and tying them around ourselves.

That's cross-country skiing on hilly, wooded trails. For downhill skiing on an open slope, you'd probably want more face protection and sun protection. (But then you have to pay more for downhill skiing, so if you're going to start, opt for cross-country.) Our skis, boots and bindings are secondhand. Our pin-style bindings are not the latest, but they worked fine for everybody just a few years ago.

In summer we enjoy canoeing and fishing. When we started to fish, not knowing if we'd like it, we got cane poles (less than $5 for a complete outfit). Over the years we've gotten several inexpensive rods and reels. Our secondhand canoe was a bigger expense, but we got it by watching the ads in the local shopper's guide and making a fast phone call. When you're not rich, you have to be clever.

TO LIVE
IS TO LEARN
32

*T*hough you may be reading this because you're a student on a tight budget, it's more likely you've been out of school for a while. It is also likely that school wasn't much fun—at least the studying part wasn't fun.

But now that school is behind you, and you don't *have* to study, wouldn't it be fun to learn something new?

Like what? Like just about anything. Acquire a new skill. Read up on an obscure topic you always wanted to know more about. Investigate whether you really have that latent talent you've always suspected.

Learn a card trick. Read about czarist Russia. Start playing chess. Find out about your family tree. Try to make some curtains. Get a compass and learn orienteering. Study Spanish (or French, or Arabic, or New Testament Greek). Read works by famous authors every educated person should know (but you've never gotten around to reading). Take up calligraphy. Fly a kite. Read the books of the Bible you've never read. Learn American Sign Language. Master the art of changing the oil in your car (see miscellaneous suggestion #41).

You can learn things from the library, from summer recreation programs, from other people who are glad to show you. As Yogi Berra said, "You can observe a lot by watching." If you can hang around somebody who knows how to do something, you'll pick up a lot.

JUST RELAX
33

*D*o you remember lying in the yard in the sun looking up at the clouds, doing *nothing but* looking at the clouds? Those were unplanned, unscheduled, unprogrammed times of childhood. Weren't they some of your best times? Today's children are supposed to be ecologically conscious, but you wonder—as they run from gymnastics to hockey to Little League to Japanese lessons—do they even notice there are clouds?

What's wrong with doing nothing for entertainment? Or doing as little as possible? Sitting at home with the radio on, sitting by water even if we don't own a boat, sitting by a window watching who and what goes by?

Are we too afraid of silence? Do we fear inactivity? Are we

nervous that someone will think we're unproductive?

We heard about a woman whose life was so harried that the only way she could escape was to put on scuba-diving equipment and sit in the bottom of a swimming pool. That was her way of getting away from it all and doing nothing. Since it's expensive to take scuba-diving lessons or put a pool in your backyard, try lying on your back and looking up at the clouds, which are free.

SLIDE SHOWS
34

*I*t seems most people take color prints, and fewer and fewer people take slides. Consequently most of the slides people have around the house are old. Invite your friends to bring some of their slides for a slide night. Not only will you laugh at each other's looks from years ago, you'll discover things about each other's history you never knew. One friend showed battlefield shots of the Korean War!

Those jokes about falling asleep during slide shows have some roots in reality. It's a good idea to limit the number of slides per person (try ten). Give each person time to explain what you're seeing, but take charge of the projector yourself so you can keep the slides moving.

If you don't have a screen, it's possible to improvise. At our house we project slides onto a window shade which pulls down over the large front window. Of course that means anybody going past the house can see the pictures from the street (in reverse). We haven't yet found the neighbors gathered in their lawn chairs eating popcorn and watching the show. Maybe that's because in northern Wisconsin we have to show slides in winter, because in summer it's light till 10:00 p.m.!

For your gathering, serve one of those inexpensive snacks mentioned in the food section of this book. Or ask people to bring a favorite snack. People are not offended by this request. There are folks just dying for an excuse to make their Double Choco-Fudge Mystery Delights, but if they make them for themselves, they'll eat them all.

A slide night is also an enjoyable party for a small church, or for a larger church if you limit each person to two or three slides. Our fellowship is helped when we understand each other better, and one way to understand each other is to understand more of each other's histories. A slide night would be a great way for newcomers and longstanding church members to get to know each other.

Of course you can have your own family or individual slide night too. Dust off those slides you haven't seen in years and enjoy them. Maybe your own kids have never seen them. Instead of delivering a dry lecture about each picture, ask the kids to guess or make up stories about what they're seeing, before you tell them the real story.

Geographic idiosyncrasy note: Up here sledding is called "sliding," and some people mistook our first "slide night" for a sledding party. Fortunately we corrected it before they showed up with their sleds and stocking caps!

When You Give, Give Yourself First

Sometimes, simply because they love God, the people suffering the most financial hardship become the most generous givers. Paul said of the Macedonian believers:

"Out of the most severe trial, their overflowing joy and their extreme poverty welled up in rich generosity. For I testify that they gave as much as they were able, and even beyond their ability." Why were they willing to do this? Because "they gave themselves first to the Lord" (2 Corinthians 8:2-3, 5).

You may discover that now you always remember to bring canned goods for the church food shelf. That's because you know how it feels to wonder if there'll be enough money for food.

You may find you're more loosely attached to things and can give them away more quickly to those whose need is deeper than yours.

You may wake up one morning and realize you're contented with life—perhaps more contented than when you had more money.

FOR THE LOVE
OF IT
35

*T*he high quality of amateur arts and entertainment in our town often amazes people who move here from the city. It's good partly because people in any isolated area have a history of making their own entertainment, partly because this area attracts artistic people, and partly because many amateurs—when they are given the opportunity and freedom to do what they do—are as good as professionals.

In any community there are people who are very good at what they do for fun. Many have the sheer talent and ability to do for a living what they love to do in their spare time, but their life circumstances or lack of drive or interest kept them from it.

These are the true amateurs. The term *amateur,* which

unfortunately has come to mean "somebody not quite competent," comes from the Latin for "love" and means "someone who does something for the love of it."

Don't spurn amateur events as inferior entertainment. Go watch people doing what they love to do. Whether it's softball or bluegrass music or acting or folk dancing, dedicated amateurs will always put on a good show, and the ticket prices will be reasonable. Unlike a lot of professionals, they will also mingle and talk to you after the show. Why not? They're your neighbors.

But why just watch? Get involved doing what you're a dedicated amateur at doing, and you'll never be at a loss for entertainment.

Some of our most engaging times have come from our involvements in community theater. We have acted, directed, designed and built scenery, written scripts, done publicity, recruited actors, run the lights, taken and developed pictures, cleaned the theater bathrooms, and just about everything else involved in putting on plays. We see amateur actors and artists, when they believe in what they are doing and have the basic ability to do it, going about their work with a single-minded professionalism—though the most they'll get out of it is a pizza party after the last performance.

Amateur sports probably accomplish the same ends and call forth the same serious purpose in the players, but since we're into the arts rather than sports, we can only tell you about our own experiences. One thing is certain: no one involved in this kind of do-it-yourself entertainment ever has to be bored.

FREE
TIME-FILLERS
36

*O*ur newspaper has a section called "Area Reports" where all sorts of organizations announce their public events. This week you could go to a pancake breakfast to benefit a youth scholarship fund, an art exhibit of checkerboard-pattern drawings, a free movie with popcorn, a political potluck buffet, a square dance, a lecture on mental health in Indian adolescents, a polka dance and potluck, and a historical society meeting. That doesn't count the special events for seniors or children and the "members-only" meetings of particular organizations. (There are also several other benefit dinners and lunches for various causes, but we don't want you to think all we do up here is eat.)

This week's events in our community reflect our area's

cultural history and current concerns. They might not interest you, but what matters is that they are opportunities for people to get together—often learning something or contributing to others in the process—and they're all either free or cost under $5.

> **Fun, Not Fanatical**
> Living cheaper is a good and necessary practice; it does not have to become a fanatical religion. You don't need 100 percent compliance with "cheaper" in all areas. In fact, an occasional indulgence becomes affordable because you have saved in so many other areas.

Your own local paper or posters around town will tell you about things you can do for free or for next to nothing. They might include outdoor concerts, school plays, school sports, workshops, art exhibits, or just about anything, depending on your area's interests.

Of course you don't have to rely on someone else putting on a free event. Picnicking, walking, biking, reading, visiting friends—they're all low-cost or free.

THE LIBRARY
37

While the last thing we want you to do is stop buying books, we must mention the value of your public library as a source of free entertainment for you and your whole family. Here are some of the resources you can find there:

Books, of course. Though your library may have a small collection, you aren't limited to what you see on the shelves. The resources of hundreds of other libraries are available to you through interlibrary loan. A title, an author, or even a general subject can start a computer search, which often brings you just what you're looking for.

Music. It's risky to buy recordings without having a chance to hear them first, but at the library you can borrow tapes, CDs and LPs and enjoy them at home for free.

Videos. While commercial video rental is inexpensive entertainment, borrowing from the library is even cheaper: free.

Magazines. Even if you decide to save money by not renewing some of your magazine subscriptions (see #48) you may still be able to read them at the library. You'll find current issues of all the popular magazines and many specialized magazines you didn't know existed.

History. Since history depends on someone tending accurate records of the past, the public library is usually a center for the local historical society's programs and displays. Even small-town public libraries often have a fine little museum tucked away in the basement or upstairs. There you can find out a lot about your community and state—how you got where you are and where you might be heading.

Discussions, programs, meetings, presentations. Take a look at the posters tacked up at your library. You may find an upcoming book-discussion group, a children's clowning workshop, a forum on ecology, a series of talks on women artists, an evening with someone who just spent a year in Afghanistan— and you can never tell what else.

If you take your children to the library and make it a positive and enjoyable time, you'll give them a wonderful lifetime gift. They'll learn how great a community resource a library is, and they'll grow into enthusiastic library users—and supporters.

THE ART OF
CONVERSATION
38

*F*or entertaining evenings, consider starting a salon.
(That's salon, not saloon.)

If the proliferation of support groups tells us anything, it
says that Americans feel a terrific need to talk. And no matter
how busy they are, many will take the time to talk if they are
given the chance.

But at this point we're not talking about support groups as
such. We're talking about groups of people just conversing
about all kinds of interesting ideas.

The "salon" was originally a reception room in a large
house, the place where guests gathered. In the seventeenth
and eighteenth centuries in Europe, the "salon" became the
gatherings themselves. At each salon you would find the

members of society whom the hostess found most fascinating: artists, political movers, innovators, anybody who had something interesting to say.

Your home can be a meeting place for ideas, or more accurately a meeting place for people with ideas. We are not talking about support groups for specific problems, just gatherings of people who think and who like to talk about what they're thinking. This doesn't require a lot of complicated planning. Invite some interesting people—maybe a combination of people you know well and people you don't—and ask them to come over for some snacks and a visit. Don't formally tell them you're asking them for an evening of stimulating conversation. They'll think either that you're starting some kind of support group or that every word that comes out of their mouths has to sparkle. Keep asking interesting combinations of interesting people, and your home may become a twentieth-century salon.

Miscellaneous
V

*S*andy's favorite cookbook has a section entitled "strays and oddballs." That might label this section. Many good practical ideas don't neatly fit into housing, food, clothing, or entertainment, but we still want you to know about them. For example: general shopping, pedestrian power, tricks to fool the eye, car maintenance, plastic, shopping habits, resources, and making money off things you don't need. So here are additional, nonclassified ways to live well while living more cheaply.

TREASURES IN "TACKY" PLACES
39

*O*ur friends' son's first birthday was coming up, and we didn't have much money to spend on presents. Sandy went into a store, which will be nameless, but which is generally considered lower-end merchandise. Some would call it tacky. There she bought a small soft duck toy and hoped it would last at least a few months.

Not only did the duck survive that little boy's love; when his little brother came along, it became one of his favorite toys too. The duck eventually disintegrated in the washing machine about the same time the family moved to a different house. There was something of a family crisis when the boys realized it was gone. "We want to go back to our old house," they kept saying, "and find our duck."

In the meantime, the tacky store had gone out of business; its shelves were duckless. Finally Mom found sort of a replacement duck from a "real" store. He's bigger, but he doesn't have that certain something.

Tacky stores can contain hidden treasures, not only for gifts but for things for yourself. One of our most beautiful accessories, a brass letter-holder, was bought at that same store. Under that avocado tree we told you about, a graceful paper parasol fills one corner of our living room; it came from a chain discount store.

Another sort of tacky-looking store which can be a gold mine is the salvage store. Their merchandise, which is all new, consists of whatever the store owner has managed to buy recently. It may come from a split-open truck trailer or a derailed freight car. Salvage stores deserve regular visits because you can never tell what will turn up. Twice when we needed large amounts of unusual fabric for theater projects, we found exactly what we needed at a salvage place for $2 per yard.

FLEA MARKETS
40

*A*ccording to *Smithsonian* magazine, more than a million Americans spend part of each year selling things at flea markets. Nobody knows how many people spend an equal amount of time buying things at flea markets.

Don't let the name "flea market" bother you. The name began in France (*marche aux puces*) as an acknowledgment that some of the clothes and bedding offered at ancient bazaars really did come complete with parasites. The term was brought to America by postwar tourists, and flea markets began to catch on here in the late 1940s and early 1950s.

Loosely defined, flea markets are where vendors sell anything and everything, most of it old, some of it new. They may be permanent places of business or one-time annual events, bringing nomadic vendors from all over the country. They may be indoors or outdoors. Some small local flea markets are nothing more than group garage sales or sales to benefit a church (like the Holy Family Flea Market where we got our wool Oriental carpet). Most fun are the ones where the vendors go to flea markets as their main occupation or weekend avocation; they are knowledgeable about the history of their stuff and love to talk about it.

What can you find at a flea market? This book isn't large enough to contain the list, but the person determined to live on less will find help here in the form of tools, chairs, toys, lamps, china, mirrors, glassware. Just about anything found at a flea market could be used as a decorative item and a sure conversation-starter.

Prices at flea markets are usually negotiable. Start by assuming the vendor has priced an item higher than he or she will expect. Decide the maximum you're willing to pay, then offer a lower amount. (You just might get it for that!) If the vendor is not playing hard-to-get, you will probably be offered a price in between. If you run into a tough one, you might wander off for a while, come back later and offer a compromise price. As with garage sales, you'll often do well by stacking up several items and offering one price. Vendors want to keep quantities of merchandise moving.

If you're embarrassed that you acquired something at a flea market (though you shouldn't be), you don't have to be specific about where you got it. It's enough to say "at a place I ran across" or "on a trip." Considering the growing popularity of flea markets, you shouldn't have to feel shy about patronizing them. You're part of a growing—and smart—crowd of money-savers.

Flea markets are so much fun that they deserve a warning

label: If you start buying things you don't need just because they're cheap, you're not really saving money. Go with some specific objectives in mind ("I'm looking for some quart jars and an 18" x 20" picture frame") and set your spending limit in advance.

CHANGE YOUR OWN OIL
41

*M*e, change my own oil? No way!" Do you remember crawling under the car with the old two-handed grease gun, struggling to force grease into a frozen fitting while trying to wipe sand out of your eye with a greasy hand?

If that's still your image of the "lube job and oil change," you've lost touch with the modern automobile. Those grease fittings are long gone, and with some of today's cars you can change the oil in a white shirt. It's probably best, however, to wear an old shirt the first time. Some cars are easier than others.

Check your car manual to find out the kind of oil to buy, how much you need, and how often you need to change it. That warning about changing oil more frequently if you "operate in extreme conditions" doesn't just mean driving in the hot desert. If in the winter your car's engine barely gets warm before you shut it off again, that's one of the most severe driving conditions possible. The heat in the cold engine will be just enough to produce water vapor in the oil. If short trips are your pattern of winter driving, you'll need to change oil more frequently than your manual recommends.

Most larger discount stores sell both oil and filters for much less than service stations. Hanging near the filters you'll find a book telling which filter fits your car or small truck. The book will also tell you which air filter, fuel filter and various other filters fit your car.

Unless driving in your area is very dust-free, you'll probably want to change the air filter while you're at it. You'll find it in the large round container on top of the engine. There will be a thumb screw and maybe some side clips holding it together. Check it by removing the old filter and holding it up to the light. If you can easily see light through the filter, it will last until the next oil change.

When I change the oil in our 1986 Nova, I just drive one of the front wheels up onto a short length of two-by-six to raise the front end enough to get a container under the drain plug. The first time, you may wish to use portable car ramps so you can crawl under the car to see better. *Set the emergency brake and block a rear tire!*

The oil drain plug will no doubt be located on the lowest part of the back side of the engine. It's the nut that doesn't look like it's holding anything. Place an empty container under it and remove the plug, using a wrench that fits snugly.

While the oil is draining, find the oil filter. It looks like a white or orange vegetable can fastened to the side of the engine. It unscrews by turning it counter-clockwise (you may need a special oil filter wrench), but don't remove it yet. Wait until the oil has finished draining from the oil pan, replace the oil drain plug, then put the same container under the oil filter and remove the filter. Wipe a small amount of oil onto the rubber gasket of the new filter and screw it on hand tight. Put fresh oil in the car, start the engine, and check for leaks. Close the hood and you're finished. Pour the oil into a container, like a gallon milk jug, and dispose of it at a service station or recycling center.

Check the general maintenance section of an auto repair manual, available at your local library, and learn about several more easy money-savers you can do yourself.

SELL WHAT YOU DON'T NEED
42

*M*ost of this book's fifty ways tell you how to save money. This one actually tells you how to make money. In the process you'll help other people who are trying to live more cheaply.

You can raise some cash by selling things you don't need. You can do it through a public sale such as a garage sale. Often several neighbors or friends will be happy to go in with you and have a sale together. If you have only one or two major things to sell, put an ad in the local newspaper or shopper's guide, or thumbtack cards on the bulletin boards at the grocery stores and laundromat. You'll get responses! There are a lot of people out there like us, looking for good stuff at an affordable price.

Maybe you feel insecure at the idea of selling anything. Who knows what you or your children might need someday? If you have second thoughts about selling something, hang onto it for now and think about it. Sell things which have no practical use anymore and no sentimental value.

Of course you must ask, "No practical use or sentimental value for whom?" A toy that lies in a trunk for years may turn into your child's most prized possession when you try to put it on the garage-sale table. Someone may insist that the motor in that rusty washing machine will come in handy someday.

You'll have to judge your right to override your family's attachment to each particular item. Some things aren't worth fighting about for the sake of a few dollars. Maybe you can sell it next year. People change, and by next year that cherished item may have turned into a piece of junk.

When it comes to things you inherited or were given by family members, you may decide (for the sake of harmony) to ask all your relatives if any of them wants the item before you sell it. Or you can go ahead and sell it and take the risk.

What's good to sell? Furniture, clothing, appliances, decorative items, gifts you never liked much (if the giver is far away), outgrown toys, bicycles, books you're never going to read again. To get an idea of prices, compare with other ads or sales in your area, and don't be afraid to go a little higher, because people expect to bargain with you. (If you're immovable on the price, state the amount and add "firm.")

CONSUMER REPORTS
43

We know people who think the only way to get the best is to pay top price. That may be true sometimes, but not always. How can we judge? What we need is somebody objective to test products in all price ranges and see whether most expensive is really best.

Someone does just that. *Consumer Reports* is a monthly magazine published by the nonprofit organization Consumers Union. It reports the results of their tests on all kinds of products and services, and they seem to delight in setting up the most fiendish tests possible. They accept no advertising or product samples and don't allow advertisers to use their findings for commercial purposes.

Each *Consumer Reports* article starts with a general discussion of the product, often including the fascinating history of how American consumers came to want it. The testers explain their methods and rationale of testing. Then comes a detailed but understandable chart comparing various features of various models, with special comments about individual models.

Consumer Reports has an iconoclastic streak and is never in awe of brand-name reputation—traits we can all use if we're going to live cheaply in our ad-saturated society. They often find more expensive products inferior to less expensive, which is reassuring for those of us who can't afford "the finest." On the other hand, if the high-priced brand shows itself superior, they let you know.

We don't read *Consumer Reports* magazine regularly since we aren't high consumers of new products and services. We do pick up their annual paperback *Buying Guide*. (You may find it at your library.) It includes a collection of recent articles and an index for the preceding five years of the magazine. So if you're shopping for a microwave, you can find out the most recent date Consumers Union rated microwaves and get that article from your library. Older reports are useful for buying a used item and for products that haven't undergone much innovation recently.

The used-car section of the yearly *Buying Guide* could ultimately save you the most money. It provides detailed repair records for the preceding five model years of hundreds of domestic and foreign cars. It also summarizes testers' responses to the previous year's models as used cars.

Aside from saving you money, the most fun thing about *Consumer Reports* is that it's so well written. Take this from an article on walking shoes from the 1991 *Buying Guide:*

Today, there are some 250 models of walking shoes on the market—many of them touted as triumphs of technology, and sounding as complex as NASA's moon boots. . . . But instead of trying to educate ourselves in the arcanum of a new branch of learning, we decided that the best way to evaluate walking shoes might be to have people walk in them.

According to the 1989 guide, "Anyone who has trouble distinguishing between image and reality should go shopping for frozen dinners." If nothing else, when you're feeling sorry for yourself because you can't go out and buy everything in the mall, you can curl up with *Consumer Reports* and enjoy a good laugh.

DISGUISE GENERIC PRODUCTS
44

*W*hile some brand-name products are worth the extra price, there's often a negligible difference between the store brand and the higher-priced name brand. In the case of some items like liquid bleach and aspirin, the active ingredients are identical.

Yet we Americans are fiercely loyal to our favorite brands. In certain tests, more people recognized a particular product logo than recognized a picture of the president. People wear their favorite cola or beer logos on their clothes, thus willingly serving as unpaid billboards. It's no accident that brand names inspire such devotion; advertisers aim as much at keeping buyers loyal as at winning new buyers.

So if you're a brand-name loyalist, you probably hate the

idea of seeing generic products around the house, no matter how much money they save for you. We admit it, generic and store-brand packages are usually homely. Who wants to face a pile of laundry with only a stark black-and-white box of laundry soap instead of those cheery blue-and-yellow swirls? What's the fun of opening the cupboard and facing a line-up of jars with unsightly labels and names like "Valu-Rite," "PriceSavr" and "Shur-Valu"?

There's a psychology to this. Do you notice what gives high-priced name brands their high-quality feel? Often it isn't so much the contents of the container as the container itself. The packaging, not the product, is pizzazzy or comforting or luxurious or friendly or fun.

So buy one particularly attractive package of something high-priced, then when it's used up, buy the generic and put it into the luxury package.

Honest, this works (though obviously it works better with things like shampoo and dishwashing liquid than things like toothpaste and pop-up tissues). The quality of the generic is usually close to the name brand—sometimes better—and you still get to handle the familiar package and feel like you're using the high-priced item.

See? You get the best of both worlds.

MAKE
THINGS LAST
45

*D*id you know that if you unwrap your hand soap before you put it on the shelf, it will last longer? Apparently, in the open air it dries out a little so it doesn't dissolve as fast when you use it. Once unwrapped, oval bars don't stack as well as oblong ones, so if you buy a lot of the oval bars at once, don't try to stack them or you'll have a soap cascade every time you open the cabinet.

It seems like a trivial item—making soap last a little longer. But there's a principle here. The longer you can make something last, the less often you have to spend money to replace it.

For example, vacuum cleaner bags, whether upright or canister type, can often be made to last longer if you cut them open, empty them out, fold over the cut ends and staple them shut. An American wartime slogan was "Use it up, wear it out, make it do, or do without." The motto was effective for conserving resources because people had a cause: defeating the enemy. Well, you have a personal cause (living on what you've got) and you have an enemy to defeat (feeling deprived and victimized). If you can make that motto yours in a positive sense, the resources you have will stretch further than you thought possible.

Neither Honor nor Shame

When we're trying to live more cheaply, there's a temptation to turn the effort into a badge of either honor or shame. Living cheaper does not have to become a crusade. Neither does it have to be an embarrassment.

You don't have to announce to everybody—or anybody—"We're living on a shoestring." Just do it. Most people are too busy checking their own shoestrings to notice yours.

KNOCK IT OFF
YOUR LIST
46

*S*everal years ago, as an experiment, we stopped buying paper towels. As far as we can tell, our household has suffered no damage or trauma because of this decision. There were so many rags around the house that there were plenty for the jobs paper towels used to do.

In fact Sandy noticed that a lot of those rags were under-shirts of Dale's, some of them not very old, which had developed holes. The holes looked like bleach damage. She decided to stop buying bleach. The T-shirts last longer now, which means that we don't accumulate rags quite as fast, but so far we haven't had to resort to paper towels again.

All this evidence points to a conclusion: You may be buying things simply because you've always bought them; with a little

> Two things I ask of you, O LORD;
> do not refuse me before I die:
> Keep falsehood and lies far from me;
> give me neither poverty nor riches,
> but give me only my daily bread.
> Otherwise, I may have too much and disown you
> and say, "Who is the LORD?"
> Or I may become poor and steal,
> and so dishonor the name of my God.
> (Proverbs 30:7-9)

experimenting you could find they aren't necessary after all.

When you stop buying something, you automatically have more money to spend on something else. It may not seem like much, especially when it involves such trivial items as bleach and paper towels. But knocking a few things like that off your shopping list could easily save you a hundred dollars from January through December, and wouldn't an extra hundred dollars come in handy right at Christmas?

GIVE YOUR CAR
A REST
47

*F*or four weeks one summer our church had a pastoral exchange with a church in Scotland. The wife of the Scottish pastor who came to be with us always walked home from church pushing their baby in a stroller. She was surprised that she seldom met anyone else out walking, because it was so pleasant. The fact that the manse was three miles from the church, part of that up a steep hill, never occurred to her as a problem.

The gasoline that your car does not burn costs you nothing. The exercise you get walking or biking always helps you. So if there's a way to save money and get healthier, why not do it? Why not walk or bike instead of driving?

Of course there are lots of reasons for taking the car: time, convenience, bad weather, cold, heat—and mostly habit. If you're used to getting in the car for all trips, even short ones, it will take conscious effort to walk out the door, walk *past* the car, and keep walking.

Some destinations are beyond reasonable walking distance. Some loads, like a week's groceries, are hard to carry on foot. But often we take the car because we need to be somewhere and don't have time to walk. It's possible to get accustomed to leaving a little earlier.

Some people think walking is an inefficient use of time; if

If I Do It, Everybody Has To!

A certain family gives up ready-to-eat cereal and eats oatmeal instead. They save so much money that they send an extra hundred dollars a year to missions.

The experience is life-changing. They feel great about it. So they decide *everybody* ought to give up ready-to-eat cereal and send an extra hundred dollars a year to missions. How easily liberation turns into legalism. Some people who realize they can give more if they spend less immediately want to impose their discovery on others.

In moral gray areas, Paul advised "whatever you believe about these things keep between yourself and God" (Romans 14:22). Spending less and giving more should be a joyful discovery of each Christian, not a moral load of bricks dumped by one onto the other.

---

they stay home a little longer they'll get more done before the car efficiently takes them where they need to go. But for both of us, walking is also an efficient use of time. Walking gets us out of the confines of our home office and puts us back in the air and weather and sun. It provides time for good conversation while adding to our physical fitness. Walking is not only more efficient, it's a lot cheaper than driving around the parking lot of the health club looking for a closer parking space.

Even in cold weather, walking doesn't have to be a hardship; in fact if you're not used to it, the first few times you'll probably overdress and get too warm. If you don't believe it, see the discussion of skiing under "Is Special Equipment Necessary?" (#31).

MAGAZINES
48

*T*he magazines that come to our home reflect our eclectic interests. Spread out on the coffee table, their covers display everything from an ancient Roman mosaic (*Biblical Archaeology Review*) to some wildly leaping teenagers (*Group*, for church youth leaders).

It's fun to get magazines. It's even more fun to read them, but the problem is that they sometimes arrive and don't get read. That usually happens when we get too many magazines or when they no longer reflect our interests but we keep renewing them through habit.

It makes sense to get magazines that you use and enjoy. It makes less sense to subscribe to magazines you only skim and throw away or let pile up, particularly if you can skim them for free at your library.

As reading material, magazines are fairly expensive. You will definitely save money if you let a subscription expire. You'll also have to steel yourself to those heart-rending letters about how grieved they are to lose their favorite subscriber—you. Sometimes you change your mind about a magazine because the magazine changes. We subscribed to *Psychology Today* for years before it went defunct, and when it was revived in a new format, we liked it less and decided not to continue.

Some magazines are valuable to receive even if you don't read them clear through right away. Those are the magazines you keep for reference. For example, the articles in *Biblical Archaeology Review* often include meticulous accounts of recent findings and their implications for biblical history. Those are important for our work, so even if we don't read them immediately, we save them for later research.

Evaluate your magazines and decide which ones to keep and which ones to let go. You probably won't even miss the ones you sacrifice, since you weren't reading them anyway.

CREDIT CARDS
49

*I*f you can't afford to pay the full price for something, does it make sense that you can afford to pay the full price plus 18 percent interest? That's your situation if you use your credit card and don't pay the balance every month.

For the person living on a tight budget, credit cards hold out a special temptation. They promise that you can own more than you have the money to pay for. In reality, by using a credit card, you will be able to own only what you can pay for, minus 18 percent.

That doesn't mean it's never worthwhile to have credit cards. They will reduce the amount of cash you need to carry, especially on long trips. They can provide a quick emergency fund when other money is temporarily not available. But you must pay off the balance in full each month to avoid the 1.5 percent monthly finance charge. When the balance is paid off monthly, credit cards provide a convenient way of paying for shopping, bills and other expenses with only the additional cost of the small annual fee.

On the other hand, if you average a $500 monthly balance on your credit card and make monthly payments of only $50, each month you will be able to charge only $42.50 without raising your balance. Just think what that scenario could mean over a ten-year period. Say at the beginning you took your new credit card out for a $500 spending spree and made monthly payments of $50. Each month you charged an additional $42.50, while the other $7.50 went for interest. At the end of ten years you would have paid $900 in interest and had only one $500 spending spree to show for it.

If the initial spending spree isn't temptation enough, the credit card companies lure you to charge more. As long as you're making regular payments, they are likely to raise your credit line. The illusion of prosperity increases while in reality you move deeper into debt.

In modern society, credit has made a lot of good things possible. Properly used, it can provide you with a dependable car, making possible a wider selection of places to work and live. It can enable you to save on your housing costs while building equity in your house. It can even give you the opportunity to start your own business.

Credit becomes either a useful tool, making your money go further, or a slave driver, controlling your life while reducing your standard of living. It depends on how well you control your use of credit and refuse to let credit control you.

LOOK FOR OPTIONS
50

*T*his final way to live on less is really the guiding principle behind all the others. Though you've probably detected it throughout this book, it deserves to be stated separately. It's this: Always, before you spend anything, look around for other options.

For people on a tight budget, that sounds ironic. Options are precisely what you feel you don't have. But as you've surely seen by now, a budget does not have to be a straitjacket. A budget can be an opportunity for searching out other doors that are open.

Think about what you want. Now ask: What are some other possibilities of getting the same result for less money?

Just because one store has that certain item on display in

the window doesn't mean you have to walk in and buy it there for that price. You may decide to do that, but look around first. Go on an imaginative search for other possibilities. Another store may have the same thing for less, or they may have a similar thing for even less, or somebody else may be getting rid of a slightly used one, or you may be able to make your own, or you may decide you don't need it after all.

Of course, looking for options means *looking* for options; they won't always come forward and present themselves to you. You must investigate. Your investigation may be anything from glancing at the next shelf in the supermarket to asking the realtor to show you ten or twelve additional houses. You don't have to feel sorry for yourself while you do this. You're the opposite of a victim; you're taking action.

Look for options in every area of your financial life, not just for items you purchase outright. Look for a different way of accomplishing the same objective.

For example, say you'd like to do more entertaining of friends in your home. When you think of having people over, you automatically think of the way your mother or grandmother did it, with a lavish roast beef dinner and a flaming dessert. Since you can't afford to do that, you put the idea of entertaining on hold until some magic future when you'll have plenty of money. Budget rigidity says "We can't do it."

Creativity, however, says "How else can we do it?" Creativity asks, "Who says guests have to sit down to a five-course dinner? Will the sky fall in if we have a homemade pizza instead? Of course not."

The same principle is operating when you can't afford to go to a particular cultural event, so you volunteer to help put it on. You get to go, and you'll probably be welcomed at other events as long as you help a little. It's the same principle when you realize "I'm cold" and go put on a sweatshirt instead of turning the heat up. You achieve your goal by choosing an option that costs less—or nothing.

Resist feeling stifled financially. Remember that God always has new possibilities for us. His way of life is not stifling but freeing. While God is not in the business of getting us freebies, he can be trusted to provide what we need at the time we need it. That assurance, along with our trust and imagination, will keep us looking for his options for us and will help us live joyfully on whatever he provides.

Better the little that the righteous have
than the wealth of many wicked;
for the power of the wicked will be broken,
but the LORD upholds the righteous.

The days of the blameless are known to the LORD,
and their inheritance will endure forever.
In times of disaster they will not wither;
in days of famine they will enjoy plenty.
(Psalm 37:16-19)